AF110173

Learning How To See
In The Dark

Nikki Gavin

Learning How to See in the Dark
© 2026 Nikki Gavin

All rights reserved.

No part of this book may be reproduced or distributed without the author's written permission, except for brief quotations in reviews or articles.

ISBN: 9798348477103

First Edition – 2026

Seeing in the Dark

There are seasons when life doesn't fall apart loudly.

Nothing crashes. Nothing explodes. You keep showing up. You keep functioning. From the outside, everything looks fine.

But inside, something feels dim.

You don't feel broken — just tired. Not lost — just unsure. You're still doing what needs to be done, still caring, still leading, still believing… but with less clarity, less energy, and less joy than before.

This is the dark most strong people experience.

Not the kind of darkness that stops you — the kind that requires you to learn how to see differently.

For a long time, strength has been your identity. You've been the dependable one. The helper. The one who figures it out when others can't. You've learned how to navigate responsibility, pressure, and expectation with quiet resilience.

But strength without support eventually creates cracks.

This book is not about becoming stronger.

It's about learning how to see — and care for yourself — when strength alone is no longer enough.

Here, the dark is not failure.

It is transition.

It is information.

It is an invitation to stop forcing clarity and start listening more closely.

You are not behind.

You are not weak.

You are becoming aware.

And awareness is where healing begins.

Table of Contents

Seeing in the Dark iv

Chapter 1 The Strong One Syndrome 7

Chapter 2 The Weight You Carry in Silence 12

Chapter 3 When Strength Becomes Survival 16

Chapter 4 Rest Feels Like Risk 20

Chapter 5 The Guilt That Follows You 24

Chapter 6 When You Don't Know How to Be Held 28

Chapter 7 Why Rest Feels Like Guilt 30

Chapter 8 Faith, Calling, and Exhaustion 32

Chapter 9 Learning How to Receive Support 34

Chapter 10 Sustainable Strength 38

Chapter 11 Redefining Purpose Without Self-Sacrifice 40

Chapter 12 When the Strong One Is Finally Supported 42

You don't have to understand everything right now.

Sometimes awareness is the beginning of healing.

Chapter 1
The Strong One Syndrome

There is a quiet identity many people carry without ever choosing it.

The strong one.

You may not remember the moment it began, but you remember the role. You were the reliable one. The dependable one. The person others leaned on when things fell apart. Somewhere along the way, strength stopped being something you did and became something you were.

At first, it felt like purpose. Later, it felt like pressure.

Being strong often starts as survival. You step up because someone has to. You learn quickly that things move more smoothly when you handle them yourself. You notice that people feel safer when you don't fall apart. Over time, your composure becomes a comfort to others — and an expectation placed on you.

The problem is not strength itself.

The problem is when strength becomes your only acceptable state.

The strong one rarely gets asked how they are really doing. And even when they are asked, they often don't know how to answer honestly. Strength has taught them to minimize their own needs, to delay their feelings, to keep moving no matter what is happening inside.

You learn to push past exhaustion.

You learn to compartmentalize pain.

You learn to carry weight quietly.

Eventually, rest feels unfamiliar. Slowing down feels unsafe. And asking for help feels like failure — not because anyone said it was, but because you learned early on that things only stayed together when you stayed together.

This is what I call The Strong One Syndrome.

It is not a diagnosis. It is an awareness.

It shows up when you feel guilty for resting.

When you feel uneasy when things are calm.

When you don't know who you are outside of responsibility.

It shows up when strength becomes a shield instead of a support.

The hardest part of being the strong one is not the work you do for others — it is the cost to yourself. When you are always holding everything together, you rarely get the chance to notice what is quietly unraveling inside you.

But awareness changes things.

Naming this pattern does not mean you stop being capable. It does not mean you abandon responsibility or lose your reliability. It simply means you begin to see where strength has been carrying more than it was ever meant to.

And seeing clearly is the first step toward learning how to carry your life differently.

Reflection:

When did strength stop being a choice and start feeling like an obligation?

What emotions do you postpone in order to remain "the strong one"?

What might strength look like if it included honesty and rest?

Affirmation

I am allowed to be strong without being overwhelmed. My strength does not require my silence or my exhaustion.

Strength doesn't disappear when you rest.

It simply learns how to breathe.

Chapter 2
The Weight You Carry in Silence

There is a kind of weight that doesn't show.

It isn't visible on your shoulders or written on your face, but it settles quietly in your body, your mind, and your spirit. It is the weight of responsibility carried without recognition. The weight of being the one others depend on — even when no one realizes how heavy it has become.

Silence often becomes the container for this weight.

Not because you are unwilling to speak, but because you have learned that speaking doesn't always lead to relief. You've learned to read the room, to assess who needs you most, to decide what can wait — and almost always, you are the one who waits.

You carry emotional labor others never see.

You anticipate needs before they're voiced.

You hold space for crises that are not your own.

Over time, this quiet carrying becomes normal.

You stop checking in with yourself. You tell yourself that what you feel can be handled later. You convince yourself that once things settle, once others are okay, once the pressure eases — then you'll rest.

But later keeps getting postponed.

Carrying weight in silence creates a specific kind of fatigue. It isn't just physical tiredness. It's the exhaustion that comes from constantly being "on," from holding yourself together while holding others up.

What makes this heavier is that silence is often mistaken for strength. People assume you are fine because you appear steady. They don't see the mental calculations, the emotional restraint, or the moments where you swallow your own needs to keep things moving.

Silence becomes a coping strategy — but it also becomes a barrier.

When weight goes unspoken, it has nowhere to go. It settles deeper. It shows up as irritability, numbness, restlessness, or a constant feeling of being overwhelmed without a clear reason why.

And still, you keep going.

The truth is, you were never meant to carry everything quietly. Strength does not require silence. Support cannot enter where nothing is named.

Learning how to see in the dark means learning how to notice what you've been holding alone. It means acknowledging that silence may have protected you once, but it doesn't have to be your permanent way of surviving.

Light does not arrive all at once. Sometimes it begins with a single honest recognition: this is heavy — and I don't have to pretend it isn't.

Reflection:

What responsibilities do I carry that go unseen or unacknowledged?

Where have I learned to stay silent instead of expressing need?

What might shift if I allowed one weight to be shared?

Affirmation

I do not have to carry everything alone. I am allowed to name what feels heavy.

Not all growth is visible.

Some of the most important work happens in silence.

Chapter 3
When Strength Becomes Survival

For many strong ones, strength did not begin as a virtue — it began as a necessity.

You became strong because circumstances required it. You adapted quickly. You learned to function under pressure. You figured out how to keep moving forward even when things felt uncertain, unstable, or overwhelming. Strength became the way you stayed afloat.

At first, it worked.

Strength helped you survive moments that could have broken you. It gave you focus when emotions felt too heavy to process. It allowed you to make decisions, show up, and handle what needed to be done. In many ways, strength saved you.

But survival has a cost.

When strength is rooted in survival, it rarely leaves room for softness. You stay alert. You stay prepared. You stay guarded — not because you don't want peace, but because you don't fully trust it. Calm can feel unfamiliar when your nervous system has learned to stay on high alert.

You don't rest deeply.

You don't relax easily.

You don't exhale completely.

Even when things improve, your body remembers what it took to get through. Strength remains active long after the danger has passed.

This is when strength quietly shifts from a tool into a mode of being.

Survival strength teaches you to push through discomfort rather than listen to it. It convinces you that slowing down is risky, that emotions can wait, and that vulnerability should be carefully managed — if allowed at all.

You may notice yourself staying busy to avoid stillness. Or feeling uneasy when there is nothing urgent to fix. Or struggling to identify what you feel because you learned long ago that feelings were secondary to function.

None of this means something is wrong with you.

It means your strength did its job — and now it may be time to let it evolve.

Learning how to see in the dark means recognizing when survival is no longer required, even if your body still behaves as though it is. It means allowing strength to soften into awareness, resilience, and care.

Survival strength keeps you alive.

Sustainable strength helps you live.

You don't have to abandon the strength that carried you. You simply get to teach it a new purpose — one that includes safety, rest, and restoration.

Reflection:

When did strength become necessary for my survival?

How does survival show up in my body today?

What would it look like to let strength shift from protection to presence?

Affirmation

I am safe enough to soften. My strength can evolve beyond survival.

You are not behind.

You are becoming more honest with yourself.

Chapter 4
Rest Feels Like Risk

For the strong one, rest is rarely neutral.

It doesn't simply feel like stopping — it feels like letting go. And letting go can feel dangerous when you've learned that things fall apart if you're not holding them together.

Rest feels like risk because you've been the one preventing collapse.

You've learned that momentum keeps things stable. That staying busy keeps emotions contained. That slowing down invites thoughts and feelings you may not feel ready to face. So you keep moving — not because you don't need rest, but because rest feels unfamiliar.

Sometimes rest feels undeserved.

Sometimes it feels irresponsible.

Sometimes it feels like weakness.

You may notice yourself justifying rest rather than allowing it. You tell yourself you'll rest after one more task, one more obligation, one more crisis is handled. But there is always something else that needs attention, and rest keeps getting postponed.

This pattern is not a failure of discipline. It is a learned response.

When you've been relied upon for a long time, rest can feel like abandonment — of others, of purpose, of identity. You may worry that if you stop, you'll disappoint someone. Or worse, you'll disappoint yourself.

Rest also creates space.

And space can be uncomfortable when you've learned to fill every quiet moment with responsibility. In stillness, there is room for grief you haven't processed, questions you haven't answered, and exhaustion you've ignored.

So rest feels risky — not because it harms you, but because it reveals you.

Learning how to see in the dark means learning to reframe rest. Rest is not disengagement. It is not quitting. It is not neglect. Rest is recalibration.

Even faith teaches us this gently. Rest is not the absence of purpose — it is part of it. Renewal does not come from constant output; it comes from intentional pause.

You don't have to rest perfectly. You don't have to rest all at once. You simply begin by allowing rest to exist without justification.

Rest becomes safer when it is practiced in small ways — a pause, a breath, a boundary, a moment of quiet without guilt. Over time, rest stops feeling like risk and starts feeling like care.

And care is not something you have to earn.

Reflection:

What fears come up for me when I think about resting?

Where do I equate rest with failure or irresponsibility?

What is one small way I can practice rest without explanation?

Affirmation

Rest is not a risk to my life or my purpose. Rest supports my strength and my clarity.

What you've been carrying quietly still matters.

Even if no one else has seen it.

Chapter 5
The Guilt That Follows You

Guilt often arrives quietly.

It doesn't announce itself loudly or dramatically. It slips in during moments that should feel peaceful — when you sit down, when you say no, when you choose yourself. Guilt whispers that you should be doing more, giving more, proving more.

For the strong one, guilt becomes a constant companion.

You feel it when you rest.

You feel it when you slow down. You feel it when you prioritize your needs over someone else's expectations.

This guilt isn't born from wrongdoing. It's born from conditioning.

You were praised for being dependable. You were affirmed for being selfless. You were valued for your ability to carry weight without complaint. Over time, you learned that being needed felt like being worthy.

So when you stop — even briefly — guilt shows up to remind you of who you've been expected to be.

Guilt convinces you that rest is selfish. That boundaries are unkind. That choosing yourself means someone else will suffer. And because you care deeply, that belief is hard to shake.

But guilt is not always a reliable guide.

Sometimes guilt is simply the echo of old expectations that no longer serve you. Sometimes it reflects roles you outgrew but never consciously released. And sometimes, guilt is just discomfort — the unease of doing something new in a system that relied on your constant availability.

You may notice guilt surfacing even when no one has asked anything of you. It appears when you imagine disappointing someone. It appears when you consider saying no before the request is even made.

This is how deeply ingrained it can be.

Learning how to see in the dark means learning to pause when guilt arises and ask gentle questions. Is this guilt pointing to harm — or to habit? Is it guiding me toward integrity — or pulling me back into patterns of overgiving?

Not all guilt deserves obedience.

As you begin to release unrealistic expectations, guilt may increase before it fades. That doesn't mean you're doing something wrong. It often means you're doing something different.

Choosing yourself does not make you unloving.

Resting does not make you unreliable.

Boundaries do not make you selfish.

They make you sustainable.

Reflection:

When does guilt show up most strongly in my life?

What expectations have I internalized that no longer align with my wellbeing?

How might my choices change if I listened to discernment instead of guilt?

Affirmation

I am allowed to choose what supports my wellbeing. Guilt does not get to decide my worth.

Rest is not something you earn.

It is something you allow.

Chapter 6
When You Don't Know How to Be Held

For someone who has carried a lot for a long time, being held can feel unfamiliar.

Not just physically, but emotionally. Being supported, comforted, or cared for in a sustained way may feel awkward or even unsettling. You may want connection, yet feel unsure how to receive it without tension.

This isn't because you don't value support.

It's because you've learned to survive without it.

When support was inconsistent or unavailable early on, you adapted. You learned how to self-soothe, self-manage, and self-correct. You became capable — impressively so. But capability can quietly replace vulnerability when there is no safe place to rest.

Over time, you may notice yourself minimizing your needs. You say you're fine when you're not. You deflect concern with humor or reassurance. You reassure others before they have a chance to reassure you.

Being held requires trust — and trust grows slowly when you've learned that reliance can lead to disappointment.

You might find yourself uncomfortable when someone offers help without conditions. You may feel the urge to reciprocate immediately, to balance the exchange, to avoid feeling indebted. Receiving freely can feel like a loss of control.

But being held does not mean being weak.

It means allowing yourself to be seen without performance. It means letting someone stay present with you without you managing their experience. It means resting in the awareness that you don't have to be useful to be worthy of care. Learning how to be held is a practice.

It begins with small moments — letting someone listen without fixing, allowing kindness to linger, resisting the urge to rush past care. Over time, these moments teach your body and spirit that support can be safe.

Being held doesn't erase your strength.

It softens it.

It steadies it.

And in that steadiness, something new becomes possible.

Reflection:

How do I respond when support is offered to me?

What fears arise when I imagine relying on someone else?

What would it feel like to receive care without earning it?

Affirmation

I am allowed to be supported. I do not have to hold everything alone.

Chapter 7
Why Rest Feels Like Guilt

For many strong ones, rest doesn't arrive quietly.

It arrives tangled with guilt, second-guessing, and an internal list of everything that still needs to be done. Even when your body slows down, your mind stays busy — replaying responsibilities, rehearsing what comes next, reminding you of who might need you.

Rest feels like guilt because productivity has been tied to worth for a long time.

You learned early that being useful brought approval. That staying active kept things running smoothly. That stopping meant falling behind. Over time, rest began to feel like something you had to justify rather than something you were allowed to receive.

You might notice guilt surfacing the moment you pause. You think of unfinished tasks. You think of people who are struggling. You think of how much more you could be doing. Rest becomes conditional — allowed only after everything else is handled.

But everything is never fully handled.

This guilt is not a moral failing. It is a learned response shaped by expectations — some external, many internalized. It reflects the belief that your value is measured by output, availability, and endurance.

Rest challenges that belief.

When you rest, you interrupt the cycle of constant giving. You create space where there was none. And in that space, questions can arise. Feelings can surface. Needs you've postponed can make themselves known.

So guilt steps in to pull you back into motion.

Learning how to see in the dark means learning to sit with this discomfort without immediately obeying it. It means recognizing that guilt does not always signal wrongdoing. Sometimes it simply signals change.

Rest does not make you less faithful, less committed, or less caring. In fact, rest allows clarity to return. It restores your ability to discern what truly matters and what can wait.

You are not meant to earn rest by exhaustion. Rest is not a reward for productivity — it is a requirement for wholeness.

As you practice resting without justification, guilt may still appear. But over time, it loses its authority. You begin to understand that caring for yourself is not abandonment — it is alignment.

Reflection:

What thoughts arise when I attempt to rest?

Where have I learned to associate rest with guilt or laziness?

What would rest feel like if it were safe and allowed?

Affirmation

I am allowed to rest without guilt. Rest supports my clarity, faith, and strength.

Chapter 8
Faith, Calling, and Exhaustion

Faith is often where strong ones find meaning — and sometimes where they hide their exhaustion.

You believe deeply. You care sincerely. You want your life to matter. And because of that, it can be difficult to admit when faith begins to feel heavy instead of sustaining.

Exhaustion doesn't always come from doubt.

Sometimes it comes from devotion without boundaries.

You may have learned to equate faithfulness with endurance. To believe that being called means being constantly available. To assume that saying yes is evidence of trust, and that slowing down signals a lack of commitment.

But faith was never meant to drain you of life.

When calling becomes fused with obligation, exhaustion grows quietly. You keep showing up because you believe in what you're doing, even when your body and spirit are asking for rest. You pray, but you don't pause. You serve, but you don't replenish.

Over time, faith can start to feel like pressure.

You may notice yourself feeling disconnected from the very practices that once brought comfort. Words that once felt grounding now feel heavy.

Stillness feels elusive. And yet, you keep going — afraid that stopping might mean falling short.

Exhaustion does not mean you lack faith. It means you are human.

Faith does not require constant output to be valid. It does not demand self erasure. It does not ask you to sacrifice your wellbeing to prove your devotion.

In fact, faith often invites the opposite — trust that you are held even when you stop striving.

Learning how to see in the dark means learning to separate calling from compulsion. It means remembering that purpose is meant to sustain you, not consume you. That rest is not disobedience, and boundaries are not a lack of trust.

You are allowed to honor your limits without questioning your faith. You are allowed to rest without explaining yourself to anyone — including yourself.

Faith that supports life leaves room for restoration.

Reflection:

Where has faith felt sustaining, and where has it felt heavy?

What expectations have I placed on myself in the name of calling?

How might faith look if it included rest and compassion for myself?

Affirmation

My faith sustains me. It does not require my exhaustion.

Chapter 9
Learning How to Receive Support

Receiving support can feel surprisingly difficult when you've spent most of your life giving it.

You know how to show up. You know how to anticipate needs, offer solutions, and carry responsibility with grace. But when the direction shifts — when someone offers to help you — uncertainty can surface.

You may not know where to place your hands.

You may feel exposed.

You may feel the urge to decline before the offer settles.

This discomfort is not ingratitude.

It is unfamiliarity.

When you've learned to rely on yourself, receiving support can feel like stepping onto unsteady ground. You might worry about becoming a burden. You might fear losing control. You might feel pressure to immediately reciprocate so the balance feels restored.

Support can feel risky when independence has kept you safe.

You may notice yourself downplaying your struggles when someone asks how you're doing. You share only what feels manageable. You stop short of honesty because you don't want to overwhelm anyone — or reveal how much you've been carrying.

But support is not meant to be earned through collapse.

Receiving does not mean you are failing. It means you are human. It means you are allowing space for connection instead of containment.

Learning how to receive support is not about depending on others for everything. It is about allowing yourself to be held in moments when you don't need to be the strong one.

Support doesn't take away your agency.

It doesn't erase your competence.

It doesn't make you less capable.

It reminds you that strength can be shared.

Receiving begins in small ways — accepting help without apology, letting someone listen without fixing, allowing care to arrive without managing it. Over time, these moments retrain your nervous system to recognize that support can be safe and sustaining.

Learning how to see in the dark means recognizing that you don't have to illuminate every path alone. Sometimes the light comes from letting someone walk beside you.

Reflection:

How do I respond when support is offered to me?

What fears surface when I imagine relying on someone else?

What would receiving support look like if it felt safe?

Affirmation

I am allowed to receive support. I do not have to do everything alone.

Seeing clearly doesn't always mean seeing more.

Sometimes it means seeing differently.

Chapter 10
Sustainable Strength

For a long time, strength may have meant endurance.

It meant pushing through discomfort, staying composed, and handling whatever came your way. You learned how to survive long seasons without pause, convincing yourself that resilience was measured by how much you could carry without breaking.

But endurance is not the same as sustainability.

Sustainable strength is quieter. It does not rely on constant urgency or pressure. It is not fueled by adrenaline or fear of failure. Instead, it is built through awareness, rhythm, and care.

Endurance asks, How long can I last?

Sustainability asks, How can I live well?

When strength is rooted in endurance alone, it eventually becomes brittle. The body grows tired. The mind grows restless. The spirit feels stretched thin. Even the most capable people reach a point where something has to give.

Sustainable strength honors limits.

It recognizes that rest is not weakness but wisdom. That boundaries protect what matters most. That saying no to one thing creates space to say yes to something more aligned.

You may notice resistance when you begin to slow down. Old habits urge you to keep pushing. Old voices remind you of what you should be doing. But sustainable strength listens differently. It pays attention to cues instead of ignoring them.

This kind of strength allows for recovery.

It allows for mistakes.

It allows for rest without justification.

Learning how to see in the dark means learning how to build a life that doesn't depend on constant strain. It means choosing practices that replenish rather than deplete. It means letting strength evolve into something that supports you, not something that demands everything from you.

Sustainable strength doesn't ask you to abandon responsibility. It simply invites you to carry it differently — with intention, care, and compassion.

Reflection:

How have I defined strength in the past?

What has endurance cost me?

What practices could help me build sustainable strength?

Affirmation

My strength is steady, supported, and sustainable.

Chapter 11
Redefining Purpose Without Self-Sacrifice

Purpose can quietly become a burden when it is misunderstood.

What once felt meaningful can begin to feel mandatory. You may notice yourself measuring your value by how much you give, how available you are, or how many people depend on you. Over time, purpose can shift from inspiration to obligation — not because it was meant to, but because you've been carrying it alone.

For the strong one, purpose often becomes intertwined with identity.

You are the helper.

The leader.

The dependable one.

And while these roles may reflect genuine gifts, they can also limit you when they leave no room for rest, change, or vulnerability. You may feel pressure to remain consistent even when something inside you needs to shift.

Self-sacrifice is often praised as virtue. But when sacrifice becomes constant, it stops being a choice and starts becoming a requirement. Purpose then begins to demand more than it gives back.

But purpose was never meant to cost you your wellbeing.

Healthy purpose includes discernment. It allows you to ask what is yours to carry — and what is not. It recognizes that being called does not mean being consumed. That service does not require self-erasure.

You are allowed to evolve.

Redefining purpose does not mean abandoning meaning or commitment. It means allowing purpose to mature alongside you. It means releasing the idea that you must suffer to prove sincerity or remain relevant.

Learning how to see in the dark means learning to hold purpose with open hands. It means listening when your body, heart, and spirit signal that something needs adjustment. It means trusting that alignment feels lighter, not heavier.

Purpose that honors your limits becomes sustainable.

Purpose rooted in wholeness becomes life-giving.

You are more than what you do. And your purpose is meant to support your life — not replace it.

Reflection:

Where have I equated purpose with constant sacrifice?

What parts of myself have been overshadowed by responsibility?

How might purpose feel if it included rest and self-respect?

Affirmation

My purpose honors my wellbeing. I am allowed to serve without self-sacrifice.

Chapter 12
When the Strong One Is Finally Supported

There is a moment — often quiet — when something begins to shift.

Not because everything is suddenly fixed.

Not because the weight disappears overnight.

But because you are no longer carrying it alone.

Support doesn't always arrive dramatically. Sometimes it shows up slowly, in small adjustments. A boundary that holds. A conversation that feels safe. A pause that doesn't immediately fill with guilt. These moments may seem ordinary, but together they change how you move through the world.

For a long time, being supported may have felt unfamiliar or even undeserved. You learned to rely on yourself because it felt safer than hoping someone else would show up. Self-sufficiency protected you — and that deserves acknowledgment.

But protection is not the same as peace.

When support becomes consistent, strength changes shape. It no longer relies on endurance alone. It becomes steadier, softer, more grounded. You begin to notice that you are less reactive, less depleted, less rushed.

Support allows clarity to return.

You start to see where you've been overextending. You recognize patterns that once felt invisible. You become more intentional about what you carry — and what you release.

Being supported does not erase your capability.

It does not diminish your leadership.

It does not undo your strength.

It allows your strength to last.

Life after the reset is not about perfection. It's about awareness. It's about choosing alignment over obligation. It's about allowing yourself to be human — capable, faithful, and cared for.

Learning how to see in the dark doesn't mean everything becomes clear. It means you trust yourself enough to move forward gently, even when certainty is incomplete.

You were never meant to do everything alone.

Strength was never meant to isolate you.

Allowing yourself to be supported is not failure.

It is fulfillment.

Reflection:

What has changed in how I relate to strength?

What support am I now willing to receive?

What am I ready to release moving forward?

Affirmation

I am strong — and I am supported. I no longer carry life alone.

Final Reflection

Take a moment before closing this book.

What is one thing you are ready to release?

What is one way you will begin caring for yourself differently?

What support are you now willing to receive?

You do not have to rush the answers.

Sometimes the most important changes begin quietly — with a single moment of honesty.

Carry forward what resonated with you.

And remember:

You were never meant to carry everything alone.

www.ingramcontent.com/pod-product-compliance
Lightning Source LLC
LaVergne TN
LVHW092101060526
838201LV00047B/1509